Little Bits of Wisdom

A collection of tips and advice from real parents

Compiled by Josie Bissett

Illustrated by Debbie Tomassi
Edited by Dan Zadra
Designed by Kobi Yamada & Steve Potter

COM·PEN·DI·UM™
Incorporated

Publishing and Communications
Lynnwood, Washington

Acknowledgements

My heartfelt thanks to the following people and organizations:

Mom and Dad, for helping me learn and grow and for giving me the encouragement to reach for my dreams. Most of us don't realize how much our parents have done for us until we become parents ourselves. **Rob Estes,** my best friend and husband, and world's greatest daddy—there is no one I'd rather ride with on the roller coaster of life! **Jenny and Paul,** my sister and brother, for being shining examples of parenthood—and Jenny for helping create this book. **Kobi Yamada** for having faith in me and making *Little Bits of Wisdom* come alive! **Tote Yamada** for all your hard work and diligence while keeping a smile on your face and mine. **Dan Zadra,** my editor, for your tender loving care with every page. Your passion and dedication are evident in all you do. **Steve Potter and Debbie Tomassi** for the fun and fantastic design and illustration. **Joan Green,** my manager, for always believing in my idea. **Brad Small** for your thoroughness and dedication. **Deborah Warren and Ron West,** for your wisdom and advice in the early stages of the book. **Christy Estes** and your friends at **Bolger and Battle** for your help and support. **Nancy Iannios,** my publicist, for all your hard work, honesty and grace—you are truly the best! **Pam Beeks** for sharing your incredible list of resources. **Dr. Bob Friedland** for giving us hope, courage and patience. **Susanna Pryzgoda** for your continued support and care for our family. **Sherrill Carlson** for your vigilant proofreading.

For aiding in the collection of these bits of wisdom, special thanks to: BabyCenter.com; babystyle.com; The Donny and Marie Show; eNutrition; eYada.com; Fit Pregnancy; The Hollywood Foreign Press Association; InStyle Magazine; Ray Kachatorian; Los Angeles Family Magazine; Kathy Manabat; MomsOnline.com and Oxygen Network; Neutrogena; Parents Magazine; Parents Online; Franck Ragaine; Tele Star; TF1's Exclusif; Kevin Sasaki; Shooting Star; Dori Stegman; and TV Guide Online.

For all the valuable sharing and comparing, thanks to all my Mommy and Me girls and teachers: Amy Frend, Cheryl Keener, Wendy Elster, Marcy Hardart, Alison Miller, Devon Wellman, Lilly Westlin, Molly McNichols, Elizabeth Song, Aimee Bellavance, Lisa Rosenblatt, Janet Hopper, Kari Ursitti, Caitlin Villante, Shelly Breger, Karen Giffen, Jennifer Byington, Pamela Johnston, Judy Silk, Jill Stuart and Laura Thomas. You were my inspiration.

To all the parents around the world who contributed to this book, thank you for sharing your wisdom. Each piece of advice was valuable, and I wish there had been room to include them all.

Dedicated to my son, Mason Tru Estes. You have taught me the true meaning of patience, selflessness and unconditional love. Your smile makes my heart sing with joy every day!

ISBN: 1-888387-40-8

Printed in China

If we share the

wisdom of our elders

with the hearts of

our children, life will

be full of wonder,

spirit and magic.

—The Mystery Lodge Theater
in Disneyland

Dear Parents,

First comes the anticipation, the joy, the excitement—the emotions I felt when I learned I would finally be a mother. Then came the curiosity, the panic, the fear—the wonder that I experienced, realizing I was about to play a starring role in a whole new venue. I was finally cast in my most sought-after role, and this time the reviews mattered to me most.

While I was blessed with the birth of a healthy baby boy, I quickly found that I didn't automatically know how to be a parent. I instinctively knew how to love, care and nurture—I just needed to learn the best ways to keep the monsters from under the bed, the fastest way to change a squirming baby's diaper, or a good trick for preventing the shampoo from running into my little one's eyes.

I quickly began my search for baby knowledge through books, the internet and, ultimately,

through the mothers, fathers and grandparents I encountered every day.

I discovered that books offer good information, but parents offer priceless wisdom and advice. "Been there, done that" is a refrain I often heard from parents and grandparents who had gained their wisdom the best way possible— through love, patience and experience.

Listening to the mothers in my Mommy & Me Groups, along with little bits of wisdom from my own parents, siblings, cousins and friends inspired the quest to expand my search to countless other parents who have been down this path. Compiling the best of their wisdom has been a wonderful and enchanting journey. The result is the first book written exclusively by parents, for parents. God bless your little ones. Enjoy!

Josie Bissett

"Where did I come from?"
the baby asked its mother.
She answered, half-crying,
half-laughing, and clasping
the baby to her breast:
"You were hidden in my heart
as its desire, my darling.
You were in the dolls of all my
childhood games. In all my
hopes and my loves, in my life,
in the life of my mother,
and in her mother before her,
you have lived.

—Rabindranath Tagore

Babies are a nice way to start people.
—Don Herold

When I was pregnant and complaining of morning sickness and sleepless nights, I read a quote by Erma Bombeck: "Never complain and always enjoy your pregnancy. It's the closest thing to God and being involved in a miracle that you will ever encounter." The rest of the pregnancy was easier. No more complaining. I simply enjoyed the miracle at hand.

—Paulette Spagnuolo

When I was expecting, I never realized how furiously I would love this baby. From the moment I first held my daughter in my arms, she just took my breath away. When she hurts, I hurt. When she cries, I cry. When she laughs, I laugh. The thought of her brings a smile to my face. All my life I have watched parents with their children, but never imagined that being a mother could be anything like this.

—Lia

I am the mother of two boys, a 4-year-old and a 7-month old. My advice is to talk and sing to them while you are pregnant. With each pregnancy I sang a different special song to each of them and to this day their special song calms them down. Like magic, my little one starts to smile as soon as he hears it.

—Diane Viodes

When I was expecting our son, I made a point to laugh as much as possible! It was my theory that if "mom" is happy, baby will be also. This really turned out to be rewarding in three ways: I always found the funny side of things, it relieved my stress, and my son, Levi, was born (and has remained) a very happy child!

—Monique Burkett

Making the decision to have a child—
it's momentous. It is to decide forever to have
your heart go walking around outside your body.
—Elizabeth Stone

When I was pregnant, several mothers warned me, "Say good-bye to sleep." Instead, I want to say to all brand-new moms, "Babies are so precious, enjoy every waking moment you have with your little one!"

When my daughter began to cut her teeth, people would say, "Wait till she bites you!" Instead, I want to remind you, "Sure, this could be a rough time on your baby, try to give her lots of love."

When my daughter began to sit up, crawl, and stand, I heard, "Oh wait till she walks, you'll wish she didn't." Instead, I want to say to you, "Wow, look at all the new adventures your child is having, isn't it wonderful?"

When my daughter finally began to walk, I heard, "Wait till she's 2!" Instead, I want to say to you, "Just think of all the new things you'll both be learning in the months to come."

—Brandi Hasse

A four-year-old boy gazed into the crib at his newborn baby sister and whispered to her, "Tell me again what God looks like—I'm starting to forget."

—Elie Wiezcoff

My daughter, Sydni, is just 9 weeks old, and I already have some words of wisdom for expectant mothers: Try to really focus on the first few days after the birth because that's when you develop the bond with your child.

I think back on the mornings when Sydni and I would watch the sun come up through the hospital window and just sit and stare at each other's face. It brings tears to my eyes. Those first few days are probably the most precious days of my life because I spent every moment I could staring at her and thinking, "Wow, I've waited 30 years to meet you and here you are! A little person ready to grow and learn about the world. And I'm the chosen one to be your guide throughout your life!"

It was also very special knowing that the entire hospital floor was nothing but new moms all nursing and bonding with their newborns. Another baby's cry made me smile—another new mom was reaching out of bed to comfort her baby.

So, to all you new moms, I say, "Starting right there in the hospital, drink in every minute with your newborn. Motherhood is the ultimate high in life."

—Tova J. Starnes

*We never know the love of the parent
until we become parents ourselves.*
—Henry Ward Beecher

A message to expectant fathers: A reporter once asked me, "What is the single most memorable moment of your life?" The answer was easy: "There are actually TWO moments."

Seventeen years ago I was there, in the delivery room, when my wife gave birth to our son, Gus, and two years later to our daughter, Rose. With my son, I felt a physical change come over the room— I can't explain it—not just a baby, but more like a strong new presence had suddenly popped into the world. With my daughter, I was actually allowed to hold her in my hands as she came through the birth canal. Incredibly, her little eyes were open, clear, tearless and staring directly into mine. Please, if it's at all possible, give yourself the incredible gift of being at your wife's side when your child is born.

—Dan Zadra

I slept with my newborn on my chest for the first three weeks of her life. Everyone warned that it might start a bad habit, but I followed my instinct and was rewarded with a very special bond with my daughter. At two months, she still sleeps with me at times. We will look into each other's eyes and know things that no one else knows.

—Kelly Layman

11

This tip is for parents who are expecting their second child. When my older daughter came to the hospital to see her baby sister for the first time, she was delighted to see her own picture in her sister's bassinet. We told her that her new sister wanted to be able to look at her big sister all the time because it made her feel happy. This short-circuited any jealousy and it helped form a positive bond between siblings from the beginning. Today, my girls are very close.

—Tiffany Rosenblum

To get older kids ready for a new baby, let them know that this is their baby too! In the hospital, right after the baby is born, have a little treat for the big brother or sister; a coloring book or candy is okay, but look for a great T-shirt ("I'm A Big Brother or Big Sister"). At home, let them help bathe the baby, pick out baby's clothes, and decorate the nursery. Keep them involved with the whole process from the ultrasound to the hanging of the diapers. That way, they don't feel left out!

—Jenny

*Just the other morning I caught myself looking
at my children for the pure pleasure of it.*

—Phyllis Theroux

When my daughter Emily Rose and I were still in the hospital, I decided I would select one special song that I would sing only to her. I chose "My Favorite Things" from *The Sound of Music*. At first I used it to soothe her at bedtime, but I soon learned it even brought an adorable smile to her face when she was teething or gassy. This has created a very special connection with my daughter. I plan to sing her our song all the days of my life to soothe her skinned knees as a little girl and even her first broken heart as a teen. I hope she will continue the tradition with her daughter some day.

—Sarah Campbell Williams

Know that each moment of your life now counts ten times more now that you're a parent.

—Christy Peterson

Starting Now...

- ♡ Never forget the smell of your newborn baby.
- ♡ Always look upon your child with kind eyes.
- ♡ There can never be too many kisses or kind words.
- ♡ Your hands are always to be used lovingly.
- ♡ Don't just listen but really hear your child.
- ♡ Always trust your instincts.

—Rosi Green

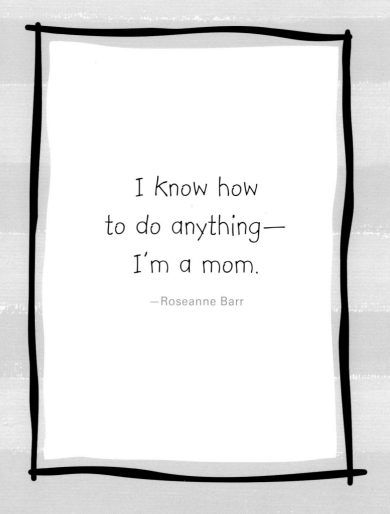

I know how
to do anything—
I'm a mom.

—Roseanne Barr

God could not be everywhere,
so he invented mothers.

—Jewish saying

Welcome to the best club in the world—
motherhood! You already know the membership
guidelines: Every day, spend good quality time
with each child and as a family. Each day give
your child plenty of hugs and kisses, and when
they get to the talking stage (even earlier), listen
very carefully to them. Talk to them, not at them.
Enjoy them while they're at play. Record all their
moments, using video, pictures, scrapbooking,
photo albums, etc. Remember that there is
nothing better than watching your beautiful baby
sleep (even though you should be sleeping too!).

—Toni Martucci

Join a mom's group right after you come home
from the hospital. In those first few months there
is no better motivation. Meeting with other new
moms on a weekly basis gives you somewhere
to go with your baby and allows you to soak up
information that you'll never find in any baby
manual. As your baby grows, the group becomes
a playgroup and your baby develops friends whom
he or she has known since birth.

—Lisa Schrader

Wisdom leads us back to childhood.

—Blaise Pascal

Listen to other mothers, but follow your heart! As a new parent you will probably receive a ton of advice. What to do, what not to do, how to get your baby to sleep all night (yeah, right!), and more. I was confused; even our two pediatricians disagreed on certain topics. Just remember, "A mother's heart is rarely wrong." If it sounds and feels right, and it works for you and your baby, it is right!

—Denise Garoutte

My name is Kitty and I'm getting ready to become a grandmom. My advice to you is no advice. Just be natural and you'll discover that you can solve almost any problem for your children. I never fed my kids any baby food. I let them sleep with the television and music on. I exposed them to people as early as one week after their birth. I read to them when they were just toddlers. I cuddled and talked to them a lot. I mostly treated their illnesses with homeopathy. I weaned them off the bottle before they were a year old. All these things came naturally, you can do it too.

—Kitty Prasad

A mother's heart is a child's schoolroom.
—Wanda Stonebraker

My advice is to trust nature—and your own gut feelings—to know what is best. Birth was around a long time before doctors made it into a medical condition. Breast-milk has been growing babies for as long as we've been on this earth. Mother's arms and breasts were here long before bottles, pacifiers, swings, bouncers, exercisers, and teddy bears with microchips that sound like a digital human heart. These are all modern substitutes (poor ones, at that) for what the baby really wants and needs—its mother and father! Parents become convinced by the retail world that they "need" all those gadgets and gizmos to be a good parent. All you really need are breasts, diapers, a sling, and a great sense of humor.

—Lisa Staubly

A simple and wonderful rule of thumb: "Nurse when they need to nurse. Hold when they need to be held. Smile when they need a smile. Sing when they need a song. Love when they need to be loved."

—Karin Nappi

*A wise mother learns each day from
quiet listening. Her parenting springs from
her children's changing needs.*

—Vimala McClure

Ask your "parent friends"—they have the answer.
This is especially true if you are preparing to have
your very first baby. My husband and I hold, play
with, change, and feed our friends' babies for fun
and practice. This way, we won't be in the dark
when we have a little one of our own.

—Susan Parsons

Because the books recommended it, I made
sure my first son was on a rigid feeding schedule
throughout his first two years. He was the
crankiest and saddest baby ever. With my second
son I am feeding "on demand" and he is the
happiest little guy you've ever seen. So read the
books, but listen to your inner voice and go with
what feels best for you and your baby!

—Buffy

Here are four magic words: "Just do what
works!" For example, are you starting solids?
Forget the whole veggies first/fruit last/no juice
routine—just do what works. Need your sleep but
the only thing that works is co-sleeping with your
baby? Do it! You have maternal instincts. Use what
you have—your wits. They're there for a reason.

—Jennifer Miller

*A grandmother is a person with too much
wisdom to let that stop her from making a
fool of herself over her grandchildren.*

—Phil Moss

The first time around my mother-in-law said to me,
"You have to get that baby on a routine, he needs
to eat and sleep at the same times every day."
Well, being the "know-it-all kid", I ignored her
advice. Looking back, my first child was not very
content. He ate and slept at different times each
day, and when he fussed I never really knew if he
was tired, hungry, or sick. With my second baby I
discovered the secret to a happy mother and baby.
Right out of the hospital I put my baby on a
schedule for eating, sleeping, changing diapers,
and play times. We both knew what to expect
each day, and we were both a lot happier.

—Andrea Brown

Every child has a built-in development schedule.
I have a son who was walking, talking, and potty–
trained before the age of one. Several years later
when I had my daughter, I expected her to be the
same as him and learn fast. She didn't and I was
disappointed at first. I checked up on develop-
mental milestones and found that she was not
behind, but right where she should be. So just
relax. Every child will develop at his or her own
rate and there's really nothing we can do to speed
it up.

—Christine Dillon

*It is thought that children acquire language
to tell the story that is already in them.*

—Anonymous

You won't find this tip in any book: The day I brought my son home from the hospital I turned on the TV, radio, dishwasher, etc. to make all the noise I could so he would not be a light sleeper. So many new parents try to be very quiet and then wonder later on why their baby wakes at every little noise. The fact is, your new baby has been in a nursery with other screaming babies since birth, so make all the noise you can the first week home and you'll enjoy the results for years to come. When you have company over, or when your older children are playing noisily, your baby or toddler will nap right through it all!

—Kimberly Hargis

Before I had children I saw the world as black and white, right and wrong. After my first daughter was born, I realized this perspective doesn't work as a parent. My advice to new moms is this: Never say never, and do what works for you! You will be more relaxed and more open to new ideas and strategies, and both you and the baby will benefit from your newly acquired mellowness.

—Tamalin Plowman

A mother understands what a child does not say.
—Proverb

One day, just after I took my baby girl home from the hospital, my mother-in-law and I were gazing at her little face as she slept in the bassinett. My mother-in-law said, "It's nice to know she belongs to you." But I immediately thought, "No, she's her own person." Although our babies are so tiny and innocent, they really are individuals and not just an extension of their parents. I have maintained that philosophy and am now watching my daughter grow into a unique and self-assured young lady!

—Helene Lohnes

As a mother of four under the age of 7, I think my greatest breakthrough came when I consciously made the decision to close my eyes, lean back, and fall into the river of their experience. If you simply abandon the need for "doing things by the book" and allow yourself to trust your (and their) instincts, true harmony ensues with your children. You can enjoy the journey, instead of wondering whether you are doing everything exactly right—or worrying if you are missing out on life while diapering or wiping tears or picking up those toys for the seventeenth time this hour.

—Anne Kennedy Luzader

My children are small, still lap-sized with
many years ahead in my care. And yet, already
I know, and I feel that one day, no matter how
many diapers changed, bottles fed, books read,
hands washed, or faces kissed, it will
never be quite long enough.

—Jennifer Graham Billings

Listen to your inner signals. On our first day
home with the baby I was so excited to see if
she would actually sleep in the bright, clean new
bassinet that I had fixed especially for her. So I laid
her in it and she started to squirm and act strange.
Something inside me told me that the scent of the
bassinet might be TOO new. Finally, I took off the
sheet, wrapped it around my tummy, and wore it
under my shirt for a couple hours. When I put the
sheet back on the bassinet, she slept like a baby.
My advice is to sleep with your new baby's
bassinet sheet a couple nights and really saturate
it with lots of familiar mommy smell!!!

—Stacey Roberts

Carrying my little girl in a sling when she was an
infant made a huge difference. I had my hands free
to do things, she loved the closeness and, if I was
really discreet, I could even nurse while walking
around!

—Sharon Reid

She made me a security blanket when I was born. That faded green blanket lasted just long enough for me to realize that the security part came from her.

—Alexander Cane

Try infant massage: A mother's touch is magic. Just holding and touching creates a special bond. I enjoyed infant massage class; my baby, Taylor, loved this special time together and the unique closeness it brought us.

—Deborah Kirkwood

Do not listen to "well-meaning" people who tell you that if you hold your child, rock your child, or play with your child too much they will become spoiled. These precious angels are only small once…take advantage of every single moment God has given you!

—Marsha Gentry

You can never spoil a baby. When a baby cries, it is because he/she needs something. For the first year or so that is the only way they have to communicate that something is wrong. Sometimes there is an obvious problem; other times they just want to cuddle. It's very important for your baby to realize that he/she can always count on you.

—Eleanor Brown

The sweetest flowers in all the world—
a baby's hands.

—Swine Burne

Go ahead and spoil your baby. During the first year give him all the attention he wants, because this is when he is learning to love and trust. While you're at it, spoil yourself too—and do it every chance you get—because you definitely will have earned it!

—Kate O'Brien

When I first found out I was pregnant, I was over the moon with excitement. Imagine this tiny person with no previous thoughts or dreams— someone who I could teach about life, love, and the world. By week two after the birth, however, I had realized that I was not the teacher. Instead, this tiny person was teaching me! Every day I was learning something new about the selfless part of life—the place where your own needs come second or third; the place where sleep is something you do in between feedings. How selfish we were with our time! I would never go back to being "just me." I love being a Mum and the daily challenge it brings to not only teach our little princess, but also to be taught by her. Enjoy every minute!

—Joanna Nido

Cherish your children while they are still breast-feeding, or on the bottle. There will come a day when they will refuse to eat anything that hasn't danced on TV.

—Erma Bombeck

My home is in my mother's eyes.

—George Nance

There is a ton of peer pressure from other mothers about breast-feeding. My advice is to ignore it. The decision to breast-feed (or not) is a personal choice, and no one should make another person feel badly either way. Some women choose not to breast-feed because of a medical condition (hepatitis C or other conditions can be transmitted to the child through breast-feeding). Others may not have produced milk or simply could not handle the pain that is sometimes associated with breast-feeding. So please don't pass judgment on new moms. Let's all respect each mother's personal choice!

—Ann-Marie Gargano

Breast-feeding can be wonderful but challenging—and I know every new mom needs all the help she can get. Right after baby comes, ask every imaginable question of the hospital nurses. Breast-feeding does not always come naturally for moms OR babies. Don't give up; stick to it, and it will get easier. The first couple of weeks are always the hardest, but soon you will experience the amazing thrill of having your baby grow and thrive from your own milk!

—Sharon Heaps

She climbed into my lap and curled into the crook of my left arm. I couldn't move that arm, but I could cradle Ashtin in it. I could kiss the top of her head. And I could have no doubt that this was one of the sweetest moments of my life.

—Dennis Byrd

I've breast-fed six children and here is my top tip. At about three weeks, start giving your baby one bottle per day (and continue breast-feeding the rest of the day). Be consistent with that one bottle... don't skip days. That way you will keep your baby comfortable with the different nipple. With two of my children, I wasn't consistent with the bottles, and ended up missing social events and feeling "trapped" because my babies would only breast-feed. With the other four, I kept them used to the bottle and I had more freedom.

—Melissa Moffitt

Make a portable breast-feeding basket! You know how it goes—as soon as you sit down to breast-feed the phone will ring. Or you'll realize that you're stuck staring at the wall for 30 minutes because the remote control is on the other side of the room! My solution? A cute basket that holds the cordless phone, the remote, a water bottle, snacks, pen and paper, reference books, my address book, thank you notes, burp cloth, etc. That way, each time I sit down to breast-feed I only have to grab one thing—the basket—to have it all.

—Jill Wilhelm

We say "I love you" to our children,
but it's not enough. Maybe that's why mothers
hug and hold and rock and kiss and pat.

—Joan McIntosh

Breast-feeding is wonderful. I could go on and on about the emotional and physical health benefits for both the mother and child. I am still breast-feeding my son (almost 15 months) and he is so healthy and happy. Breast-feeding can be challenging at first. One common complaint is sore nipples. A lot of women swear by creams that they buy, but I've found that everyday olive oil works just as well, if not better. I gave birth in Italy, and at our hospital, they advocated using it after each feeding and after showers. It really helped me. By four weeks, I felt like a breast-feeding veteran!

—Teresa Bradshaw

If you plan to breast-feed, go ahead and sleep with your baby. When she wakes up hungry at night, simply roll yourself and baby onto one side and feed her. I kept a battery-powered tap-light under my pillow so we could both see what we were doing without turning any bright lights on. When my baby was done eating she was usually fast asleep in a matter of seconds without me worrying about waking her by putting her back into a cold crib.

—Melissa Moffitt

In a child's lunchbox, a mother's thought.
—Japanese proverb

Tips for mothers who cannot or choose not to breast-feed: 1) Powdered formula is a better value than liquid, and will last longer. 2) Instead of mixing one bottle at a time, buy a 2-liter pitcher and make a big batch. Each morning pour the day's formula into individual bottles and store them all in the refrigerator until needed. 3) Do not be afraid to use the microwave, but only for a few seconds at a time. After a few seconds, pull it out each time for a temperature test. Shake and feel the side of the bottle...then repeat the process until it's lukewarm, not hot! 4) If you can afford a bottle warmer/cooler system, you can put the pre-made bottles into it and leave in the baby's room. This will save on a lot of fumbling around in the middle of the night!

—Karen Passmore

My dad installed a hot water tap (up to 190 degrees) in our kitchen. You can adjust the temperature anywhere you want it. Not only is it great for heating bottles, but we can have immediate hot chocolate or tea without micro-waving or boiling the water.

—Stacy Hathaway

A mother is a person who, seeing there are
only four pieces of pie for five people, promptly
announces she never did care for pie.

—Tenneva Jordan

My wife and I have three daughters who all eat
their veggies. Why? We think it's because their
first solid food was plain veggies. Instead of baby
food, we would often steam actual veggies and
grind them up ourselves. That saved money. Our
daughters are all about 18 months apart, very
healthy, and they are the joy of our lives (next to
God and each other)!

—Bill and Liz Darden

An easy way to cook and store homemade baby
food is to buy a packet of frozen mixed vegetables
and steam them until quite tender. Then blend
them to a smooth consistency with a kitchen wand
or blender. If the mixture is too thick, just add
some of the water you used to steam them. (You
can gradually make the mixture coarser/lumpier as
your baby grows.) Once mixed, you can place the
mixture into an ice cube tray and freeze. Once
frozen, empty the cubes into labeled ziplock bags
and store in the freezer. The cubes can then be
thawed and reheated (in the microwave or on the
stovetop) as needed. Most frozen baby food can
be kept for about 3 months.

—Andrea

As a child, my family's menu consisted of two choices: take it or leave it.

—Buddy Hackett

Label opened jars of baby food with the date they must be used by. (Much less thinking involved for a parent's overloaded brain.)

—Susan Pagano

I have a two-and-a-half year old daughter. When she won't eat, I put yogurt into the blender along with crushed ice, fresh fruit, and milk. It makes a delicious, nutritious "smoothie" and she drinks it all every time. It's much better than caving in to cookies or sweets.

—Erica Cole

Insist that your little one eat veggies, fruit, and protein, and don't avoid foods that you yourself don't care for. Give your child the chance to make up his or her own mind—and try everything more than once. My little girl makes a face at every first bite, but I tell her to try again and she almost always enjoys it. And don't feed them hot dogs, soda, french fries, etc. until they are at least 4 years old because they need to develop good habits from the beginning, and that is your responsibility. The grownup sets the rules!

—Marilyn K. Babb

The highlight of my childhood was making my brother laugh so hard that food came out his nose.

—Garrison Keillor

Children feel such a sense of accomplishment when you let them help you—even if that means it will take longer, or make a mess. Let them help you prepare dinner and you'll discover that they will give almost any food an honest try—broccoli, cauliflower, liver, etc.—simply because they prepared it. My daughter is much less "picky" when she's the one who's made dinner!

—Karen Smith

I learned this little trick from my mom. She would take raw broccoli and cut off the very tips of the florettes (so you have a bunch of teeny green balls). Then she would put them in a shaker and serve them with dinner as "green sprinkles." My son (who isn't crazy about regular broccoli) will enthusiastically shake the "green sprinkles" over pasta and many other dishes. It's a great way to add veggies to a meal in a fun way!

—Jennifer Mundy

Some of the oldest "tricks" are still the best. Our child is a very picky eater. We've learned that if she sees us tasting her food first—and enjoying it— then she will usually eat it too.

—Khadijah Theus

32

Dad showed his love by taking a wing for himself and leaving the drumsticks for us.

— Don Ward

When I first introduced my children to baby cereal, they both had trouble with constipation. I found that if I made the cereal with baby apple juice (rather than breast milk or water) the juice counteracted the constipation. This made both my children a lot more comfortable while they were being introduced to solid food. A happy baby has a happy mommy!

— Terian Johnston

When your child gets a little older, he or she will be drawn to the cereal aisle as if it were a candy store…which it almost is! Isn't it amazing how every new fad or craze eventually gets its own cereal? My kids always go for the cereal that has the most appealing box and always costs twice as much as the store brand. My solution is to buy their favorite brand once—and then refill the box with the equivalent but much cheaper store brand. My kids (ages 5 and 12) have never known the difference. It's a Win/Win. I'm happy about the cost savings and my kids get to look at their fancy boxes and the latest characters.

— Brenda Zofrea

You can learn
many things from
your children.
How much patience
you have,
for instance.

—Franklin Jones

Parents learn a lot from their
children about coping with life.

—Muriel Spark

W hen your child is first born you have every
intention of being the world's BEST mother. By
the time your child is 2, you are just struggling not
to be the world's WORST mother. Relax...take a
deep breath and know that you are neither the
world's best nor the world's worst. You are just
"Mommy", and that is all you need to be.

—Romy Allan-Windon

T he long nights, inconsolable crying, spitting baby
food, refusing to drink from a cup, saying "no, no,
no" to everything, temper tantrums, and even
refusing to potty-train all seem endless as we are
actually experiencing these stages of our baby's
life. I have begun to appreciate, however, that all
these inconveniences and frustrations are really
very small and short lived in the grand scheme of
things. As I enter each new stage with my baby,
I have come to realize that "this, too, shall pass",
and I try to enjoy these moments as they happen
because all too soon my baby will grow up and I
will ache for these stages that once drove me mad!

—Tamera Baker

Those whose homes are neat and noiseless,
generally are girls and boys-less.

—Anon

My best advice for new parents is to stop beating yourselves up when you make a mistake. The bottom line is that no bundle of joy comes with an owner's manual. We all learn from trial and error, and just when we think we have this little person all figured out, he or she is going to change the game plan. Just love unconditionally, do your best, learn something new every day, and know that everything is going to work out fine in the end.

—Ellen B. Simpson

Relax. Take every day slow, lighten up, and just enjoy your children. If they lick the slide at the playground, they will live. If they bleed a little, they will heal. Treat your children like little people, rather than little accidents or inanimate objects. So many parents worry about every little thing their children do. Hey, they are people, too, so let them be!

—Gerri-Anne Brown

Parents are not quite interested in justice.
They are interested in quiet.

—Bill Cosby

I am a survivor of postpartum depression, which eventually turned into clinical depression. The best thing I ever did for myself was get early intervention with a therapist and proper medication. Believe me, there's help out there for any mom who is suffering. Therapy is a wonderful thing!

—Jen Midkiff

Occasionally every new parent feels stressed and overburdened. At times like these, just do like the railroad crossing and STOP, LOOK and LISTEN to your little one. It will help you remember what an incredible gift God has given to you.

—Walter Hagemeier

Treasure the trying moments, even the 2:00 A.M. crying jags! Close your eyes and make a memory of how your baby looks, smells, feels, and sounds. This helps to reduce the stress of the situation and also serves as a reminder of how fleeting "babyhood" truly is.

—Jill Hayward Wagner

Being a parent means never having a minute...
yet always making a moment.
—Michael Nolan

We had a colicky son, and every family member claimed to have "the cure." Of course, none of them worked for us. Finally, our physician recommended a little bit of anise. You boil it for about one minute, cool, and give with water. It definitely soothed my son and also soothed our nerves.

—Dawn Conklin

When our daughter was 3 weeks old she developed colic. I was going crazy, so I called her doctor. He explained that colic is sometimes caused by gas trapped in the baby's abdomen. He suggested that I put her in her car seat to sleep because laying her flat on her back made the gas worse. The first time I put her in the car seat, she slept for seven hours! I kept her sleeping in the seat until she was about 3 months old and then put her in the crib. I hope it works for you!

—Marcy Green

Our son, Ryan, was very colicky. Our family doctor, who is familiar with homeopathy, suggested 2 ounces of weak chamomile tea (in addition to breast milk) each day. This really seemed to ease his stomach pain and help him relax.

—Rose

> Having a family is like having a
> bowling alley installed in your brain.
> —Martin Mull

If you're a breast-feeding mother with a colicky baby, try drinking bottled water instead of tap or filtered water. I was told that babies can't digest the fluoride in the water, even after it enters through the breast milk. I tried this and, sure enough, it worked for me and my colicky daughter.

—Tania Stepple

My husband, Mike, and I found a "miracle herb" for Brandon, our colicky son. It's called "Catnip & Fennel." We found it at the local health food store and within hours Brandon was a happy little baby. There are several ways to administer the herb, but check with your pediatrician first.

—Dawn Cone

My son, Adrian, was extremely colicky. At three months, all through the night. I thought I would lose my mind. That's when my mom and aunt came to the rescue with an old folk remedy from Colombia. Late in the afternoon they would boil some water in a huge pot and add cilantro and lettuce, which they said had a calming effect. By evening the water would cool to lukewarm and I would bathe Adrian in it. Needless to say, he did not smell that great, but he always slept better after his bath.

—Angelica Rivera

*The pressures of being a parent are
equal to any pressure on earth.*
—John Lennon

I discovered that "white noise" is a great technique for soothing a crying newborn. When my oldest son was young, we simply tuned our television set to an empty channel. He loved the "shooshing" noise. A similar effect can be obtained by tuning your radio between stations.

—Robyn Feldberg

I'm the mother of 22-month-old twin girls. If you're expecting, I suggest having one of your baby showers be a "task shower." Instead of bringing regular shower gifts, my family and friends hung a huge calendar on the wall and then volunteered their time to help me make meals for the twins, clean the house, do laundry, etc. The task calendar was a real stress-reducer and the best gift ever.

—Julie DesMarais

One thing I've definitely noticed after having my second child is that each child is unique. Just because my first child accomplished something in record time doesn't mean my second will do the same. Let your children learn at their own pace and don't push! It's less stressful for you and them.

—Denise Tudor

*Babies are always more trouble than
you thought—and more wonderful.*
—Charles Osgood

For tired new moms, remember that when
your babies keep you awake at night with their
crying, that means they are alive, vibrant, and
healthy. Remember how many nights you prayed
for their addition to your life—and just be thankful
they are here!
—Dionna Sanchez

I just want to say that no matter how bad things
may seem at times, it always passes. Instead of
focusing on life's little problems, try to focus on
life's little pleasures…your child's first smiles,
words, and steps. Watching my children grow
is the biggest reward of all.
—Elaine LeBlanc

My mother-in-law and grandma insisted I was
spoiling my kids every time I picked them up when
they cried. Maybe so, but my children (ages 6, 4,
and 2) seem to be turning out just fine. When I
think back to how fast the last six years flew by, I
am so grateful for all those long nights in the dark,
rocking my babies back to sleep. Sure I was tired,
but now I have the most awesome memories of
the sweetest times. Don't waste them!
—Lisa Kobel

41

At work you
think of the children
at home. At home
you think of the work
you've left undone.
The struggle within
yourself tears
at the heart.

—Golda Meir

Every mother is a working woman.
—Anonymous

I am a 33-year-old attorney who gave up my career to raise my two children, ages 2 and 3. My advice to all other career women is that your career will still be there, but your babies are only young once. Enjoy them when they are young and still give wet sloppy kisses.

—Meaghen Hoang

I did something that shocked me and everyone who knows me—but also made me extremely proud. I walked away from a six-figure salary and a flourishing career to raise my daughter. I had just made VP at age 29 and had every intention of returning to work in six weeks. But after meeting and falling in love with my baby, nothing else mattered more than giving her the foundation that I knew no one else could give her. Although I still feel a little strange when people ask me what I do or when I am returning to work, one look from my daughter reminds me that's she's my greatest accomplishment to date.

—Brenna Grossman Smisek

I'm a very busy working mom, and I also travel as part of my business. In the beginning I felt enormous guilt because I would see all the full-time mommies who got to spend all day with their babies. I've discovered that my son knows that I'm always going to spend quality time with him and that, even though I do go to work, I always come home. No one's situation is perfect. If you're going to work, the most important thing is to ensure that you always, always, make quality time for him.

> —Liz Lange, Designer of
> Liz Lange Maternity Wear

Being a single mom, a part-time college student, and a full-time employee, I have very little spare time. One thing that keeps me sane is to spend every spare second playing and learning with my beautiful 14-month-old daughter. Cleaning the house and homework can wait until after she has gone to bed; my baby girl needs me right now! After all, it's not the amount of time you spend with your children that matters, it's how you spend it.

> —Jacki Shill

My best creation is my children.
—Diane von Furstenberg

Combining your job or career with breast-feeding? It can be done! You just need the best double electric breast pump that you can afford. I was able to pump breast milk for my baby throughout the first year. This allowed my caregiver to feed him my breast milk while I was away at work— and then I could breast-feed him the rest of the time. It was wonderful to come home at the end of a stressful day to a baby who was waiting for mommy to nurture him—and it also nurtured me.

—Simone Thomas

Communicating with your husband and working as a team are the keys to success for working moms! I decided to continue my career after my son was born. I broke down after the first few weeks. I was doing everything—day-care drop off, office issues, household chores, cooking, etc. Help! After sitting down with my husband we decided that he would do day-care drop offs three days a week, help with household organization, and we'd ask our cleaning service to come more often. We also decided to eat take-out more often. This has helped.

—Alice Katwan

The great high of winning Wimbledon lasts for about a week. You go down in the record books, but you don't have anything tangible to hold on to. But having a baby, there just isn't any comparison.

—Chris Evert

If you must work, shop just as hard for the right daycare as you did for the right husband or wife— even harder!

—Melody Wright

The best time to shop for daycare is early on, while you're still pregnant. Many of the best ones have waiting lists. Do a thorough check, even if they claim to be "licensed."

—Kathy Barr

My daughter cried every day when I took her to daycare, but I dismissed it as "normal" separation anxiety. Eventually I discovered that she had been bitten several times, and the daycare staff hadn't even noticed! I took my Dad's advice and moved her to another daycare. What a difference! She loves these people and hardly ever cries. We really have to listen to our kids. Even when they can't talk yet, they are trying to tell us stuff all the time.

—Tammy Brown

There are homes you run from
and homes you run to.
—Laura Cunningham

My husband is a "stay-at-home-parent" which is non-traditional, wonderful, and inspirational! My advice is to remain open-minded when it comes to different parenting styles. Respect the decisions of other parents—and treasure your own choices, as they are YOURS, alone!
—Jennifer Tan

If you have to work, don't waste time feeling guilty about it. It is necessary in many cases. On the other hand, if you can cut back to part time by simply eliminating a few extras, then do it—at least until your children are in high school. Remember, our children need our presence much more than our presents!
—Kathy Barr

Every mother is a working woman. I am a mother and a fifth grade teacher. When you are feeling exhausted and doubt your adequacy, as new moms sometimes do, stop to give yourself the credit you so richly deserve. Speaking from experience, I can assure you that managing a class of twenty-eight children is much easier than being a first-time mom!
—Toni Kanes

People who say
they sleep like
a baby usually
don't have one.

—Leo J. Burke

A mother's arms are made of tenderness
and children sleep soundly in them.
—Victor Hugo

The pediatricians didn't approve, but I found a way to get my children to sleep through the night at an early age (6 weeks old)—even the children with colic! Most children go down for the night around 7 P.M., which is why they wake up at 2 A.M. Instead of letting them sleep straight through, I would wake them up at 11 P.M. and give them another bottle—one with a little baby cereal in it to fill their tummy. Then I would change them and put them back down for the night. It took a week for the routine to set in. After that, they were always good sleepers.

—Jena Carone

My pediatrician suggested that we let our infant son cry himself to sleep if he woke up in the middle of the night. If he wasn't hungry or wet we were to let our baby cry in 5-minute intervals. Sorry, but if my baby cried for more than a minute, I would start crying too. From that moment on, I decided that I would pick him up and rock him to sleep no matter how many times it took. Like my mom always told me, "Babies aren't meant to be crying, they're meant to be held." Spoiled? My pediatrician would probably say yes, but I don't think so for a minute. Secure and loved, absolutely! (By the way, he started falling asleep on his own about a month later—when HE was ready!)

—Marianne Valdes-Fauli

The people hardest to convince they're at the retirement age are children at bedtime.
—Shannon Fife

Please don't let your baby's cries in the night go unanswered. A baby "crying it out" is NOT learning to comfort himself—he is learning that no one comes for me, so I may as well give up. That's not a good association. My philosophy is, "Sleep when you're old, take care of your baby now!"

—Susan Baer

Babies always cry for a reason. They may simply want to be held, loved, cuddled, see a loved one's face, feel their touch, or just know you're there. These "needs" are just as important for your baby as good food and clean diapers.

—Julia Boone

Sometimes the old-fashioned ways work wonders. When Adam was 4 months old, we found he would wake himself up thrashing his arms. Finally, my husband tried swaddling him before we put him down for the night. To our amazement it worked like a charm! Some people think swaddling is mean to the baby, but Adam seemed comfortable and happy—and Mom and Dad got to rest too. We did this until he was 6 months old. Now Adam goes to bed like an angel.

—Jennifer Claxton Francischiello

The art of being a parent is to sleep when the baby isn't looking.

—Anonymous

Follow your baby's cues! Your little one is trying to communicate with you. If he/she is rubbing the eyes or becoming fussy, the message is probably, "Hey Mom, I need sleep." If your baby is trying to tell you that he/she needs a nap every morning after being up for only two hours—good, then make this the usual naptime. Remember, your little one can't tell time yet, and may not know that 7 P.M. is "supposed" to be bedtime. He/she may need some help winding down for the night. Try a warm bath, nursing, a story, a lullaby—whatever you both enjoy to wind down from the day.

—Denise Garoutte

Everyone told me to rest when the baby rests, and I didn't listen. Well, my advice is don't worry about cleaning—it will always be there—but rest when the baby rests!! You'll feel better each time those three-hour feedings roll around.

—Shasta Cunningham

A good rule of thumb for infants is "sleep begets sleep." Don't think that the more you keep them up during the day, the more they will sleep at night. The opposite is true. Make sure your little one gets lots of naps during the day. It will be easier for your baby to sleep at night, as he won't be over-tired.

—Jennifer Pleasants

Families with babies, and families without babies, feel sorry for each other.

—Edgar Watson Howe

My mother-in-law advised me that the easiest way to put a child down for a nap is on a full stomach. She told me to never let my son's feet touch the ground from the high chair or booster seat after finishing lunch; don't get his energy going. It works like a charm—try it!

—Vicky Stauffer

By the age of 4, my oldest son was beginning to outgrow naps, but still needed a rest. To assure some quiet time each day, I put a clock radio in his bedroom. I set the timer for one hour of soft music. He knew that he needed to stay in his bed until the music stopped. He could play quietly, or read books, but he had to stay in his bed. Usually he would fall asleep before the radio turned off.

—Kathleen Lechner

If you go into your sleeping baby's room to check on him, and find him awake and contentedly playing with his fingers, lovey, or anything else that isn't dangerous, LEAVE HIM ALONE! He'll probably go back to sleep. Don't worry, when your baby truly becomes bored or uncomfortable, he'll page you!

—Collette Book

*Cleaning your house while your kids
are still growing is like shoveling the walk
before it stops snowing.*
—Phyllis Diller

When Andrew was a newborn, I would warm
his crib with a heating pad before putting him down
for the night. As far as Andrew was concerned, a
warm crib beat cold sheets any night. He always
went right to sleep. As Andrew grew to toddler-
hood, he got weepy at bedtime. The solution was
a tape player with some Sesame Street tapes.
Contented with his music, he usually dropped
happily off to sleep. Today, at three-and-a-half,
Andrew never hassles me at bedtime, and he
actually looks forward to singing himself to sleep!

—Shannon Christensen

If the weather is hot and humid (as it is here),
and my son has difficulty falling asleep, I give him
a light massage with baby powder. This calms
him down and helps him to be more comfortable.
(P.S. Be sure to get all the creases!)

—Valerie Lees

Always make time for your baby's night-time
bath. If you add 2 or 3 drops of lavender oil, it
will soothe and relax even the most nervous baby.
When bottle-feeding, make sure that your baby is
positioned near your breast. The sound of your
heartbeat is the sweetest lullaby.

—Nina Iliopoulos

Let your little ones share a room together. When my son, Charlie, was 16 months old, our second baby, Jack, was born. For the first few months, while I nursed Jack, he slept in a cradle in our room. When it came time to move him into his own bedroom, we decided to have our little baby boys share a room.

We were a little nervous at first, fearing that Jack would wake up every few hours to nurse and disturb Charlie. The first few weeks were a little rocky, but it was definitely the right decision.

Now 25 and 9 months old, Charlie and Jack are the best of friends. Every morning we are awakened by Charlie's sweet little voice calling, "Baby Jack, baby Jack, what ya' doin'?"—and we can hear Jack cooing and giggling in response. Sharing a room gives them special time to be together. They will talk and entertain each other in their cribs for almost an hour in the morning, which also gives me quiet time to shower, dress, make breakfast, and get ready to start their day.

—Deborah Denhart

Tears suddenly come to a mother's eyes when she watches her child be happy.
—Elizabeth Jolley

Whenever my twin girls are on the verge of a meltdown, I let them run around naked while playing loud music. The girls are now two-and-a-half, and we have "naked time" almost every night after dinner—the time of day when they are getting tired and crabby, but it isn't quite time for bed. There is something about being naked that changes their mood and makes them extremely happy—and it helps me de-stress by delighting in the sheer joy on their faces.

—Kelly Mattocks

When my 2-year-old can't sleep, I promise her that after she falls asleep I will come in and check on her and put a big red lipstick kiss on her hand. That way, when she wakes up, she will know I was there and that I am just down the hall. It also helps if I leave for work before she gets up. The big red kiss assures her that I checked on her and said good-bye. Sara is the best thing that ever happened to me and I just try to do everything to make her comfortable and secure.

—Julia Newton

Recall as often as you wish;
a happy memory never wears out.
—Libbie Fudim

As a mother of three children (ages 8, 7, and 4), I have found a great way to deal with bedtime jitters or nightmares. My solution is to spray a few drops of my perfume on each child's pillow at bedtime. I tell them that the bad dreams will stay away because they will smell my perfume and think I am right there with them.

—Lisa Helton

If they are worried about monsters, use a spray bottle filled with water as "Monster Spray." At bedtime, spray under the bed, in all the closets, and anywhere else that monsters hang out.

—Kellie Tabor

Whenever my children had a nightmare and couldn't get back to sleep, here's what I would do: Blowing on their forehead swept away the bad dreams, and a light kiss on their forehead filled it with happy dreams. Now every night all my children make sure they get a "happy dream kiss" before they fall asleep.

—Kathleen Lechner

Believe me, when I was five years old I could read my ABCs. I could count before I could even go to school. Guess who I got it from? My mother.

—Ray Charles

A visit from the Pacifier Fairy: To get rid of the pacifier, put all your little one's pacifiers in a little box under his pillow and tell him that the Pacifier Fairy will take them to the little babies who need them. In exchange, the Fairy will leave a toy under the pillow.

—Kellie Tabor

We tried all the "typical" methods to persuade our son to let go of his pacifier (including cutting off a little piece of the nipple every night), but we finally succeeded with a simple bedtime story. The story was about Prince Noah (my son's name). One day Noah was walking through the forest with his friends and he dropped his pacifier and couldn't find it. His mom was calling him so he had to go home without it. That night Prince Noah had to sleep without it. It was hard, but he awoke to find he didn't need it anymore. Believe it or not, we told this story to our Noah for two nights and on the third day he told us he didn't need it anymore. No tears, no fighting, and no requests for it back!

—Andi Tye

By the age of 3,
our son had
learned to go to the
bathroom in every
room of the house,
EXCEPT the bathroom.

—Frank Langello

Never give up on a child.
—Patricia Willis

There comes a time when changing your son's diaper becomes almost impossible—wriggling, squirming, flipping over, and making terrible poopy messes in the process! The constant struggle to get him to "lie still" was wearing me down—but I came up with a game that solved the problem. I began to ask him questions like, "Can you show me where your belly button is? Where are your ears? Where is your nose?" He was so interested in helping me find his body parts, he completely forgot about having his diaper changed!

—Michele Katcher

I am the mommy of two fabulous little boys who are are only 22 months apart. When I brought the new baby home, I was overwhelmed with the constant diaper changing of both boys, so I set out to do the impossible by potty-training a 24-month-old boy. Of course, none of the usual techniques worked—so I decided to trick him. One day I pretended to put his little brother on the potty and, of course, the older brother wanted nothing to do with someone else on HIS potty. From that moment on, my older son was potty-trained.

—Mellisa Rush

*Parenthood remains the greatest
single preserve of the amateur.*
—Alvin Toffler

No child has ever been successfully "yelled" into potty-training. My two earliest memories occurred when I was about two-and-a-half—and they are still very vivid. First, I remember huddling in my mother's arms during the great Seattle earthquake. Second, I remember my Dad yelling at me for pooping in the neighbor's dog dish instead of my baby commode. Obviously my Dad's yelling fit was just as traumatic for my little mind as an earthquake. Think about that the next time you're tempted to lose it with your little guy.

—Leo Makowsky

As a mother of six, my advice is to let each child take potty-training at his own pace. The more you stress, the more they will. Trust me, between the ages of 2 and 3 you will see progress—and then one day it will just "suddenly happen"…and that will be that. Positive rewards also help, but be sure to designate those particular rewards for "potty only."

—Colleen Davis

Bonus Tip: Boys especially enjoy target practice with a few Cheerios to sink in the toilet!

—Donna Sher

Children are to be treated gently.
They are like snowflakes—unique,
but only here for a while.
—Don Ward

We have found a simple way to ensure that our young boys wake up "dry and proud." Before my husband and I go to bed at night we gently wake each of our boys, take them into the bathroom and stand them in front of the toilet. After they go, we carry them right back to bed, give them a kiss and some praise, and tuck them in. In the morning there are no sheets to wash and, most importantly, they are proud of themselves.

—Jenny Knorr

For a bed-wetting 3- or 4-year-old, use a waterproof crib pad on TOP of the sheet.

—Patricia Notholt

Our 2-year-old used to fuss the moment I tried to lay him down for a diaper change. Now I just lay the changing pad and diaper on the floor and say to him, "Want to come help me change your diaper?" Becasue he's making the decision himself, he immediately lays down and blessedly allows me to change him, fuss free!

—Mona Barry

All kids are gifted; some just open their packages earlier than others.
—Michael Carr

I am a mother of twins. Diapers got quite expensive for two, so I potty-trained as early as possible by using a doll. I simply set the doll on the toilet seat, poured water between the doll's legs, and let the girls flush the toilet. We would clap our hands when the doll went to the potty. After a few times with the doll, I would do the same procedure with my twins, including pouring water between their legs. It worked! They couldn't wait to go potty. I had them trained in just a few days.

—Sharon McMahon

If you're having difficulty potty-training, here's my mother's advice: Let your child run around naked from the waist down whenever possible. Sure, you'll get funny looks from the UPS guy, and I guarantee that you'll have an occasional "accident" on your floors, but your child will train at warp-speed. It'll be easier for him to recognize the sensation associated with going to the bathroom if he's unhindered by underwear or training pants. They are designed to be so absorbent, it's difficult for your child to know whether or not he's even gone, so he won't recognize how it feels when he has to go.

—Collette Book

Childhood is short;
regret nothing of the hard work.
—Doris Lessing

Hope for late bloomers: When my son was three I learned that potty-training doesn't train the child, it trains the parents. It trains us to sit our child on the potty every hour—and nothing gets accomplished. My son was feeling pressured and having countless accidents, and I was getting stressed. We both felt like failures. I put him back in diapers and we called it quits for a time. Three months later he started preschool and they were very strict about children being able to use the potty. I fudged and sent him in disposable underwear (Pull-Ups) because I knew he could stay dry for two or three hours. We made it through the whole year and no one knew the difference. Lots of parents do what I did, but no one wants to admit that their child is not potty-trained yet for fear of what the preschool will do. Anyway, one month after his fourth birthday we bought some cotton training pants with race cars on them, and my son immediately began to use them and the potty.

Moral: Relax and be patient. When it comes to walking, talking, or using the potty, you really do have to wait until your child is ready. When they get it, they get it!

—Patricia Jensen

The most important thing a father can do for his children is to love their mother.

—Theodore Hesburgh

*The best security blanket a child can have
is parents who respect each other.*
—Jan Blaustone

Parenthood is the most dramatic change you
and your mate will ever go through. Make sure,
from the very beginning, that you make time for
yourselves. "Couple time" will keep your marriage
strong and make you better parents.
—Theresa A. Cochrane

In the midst of wiping noses, changing diapers,
and doing the one-millionth load of laundry for the
day be sure to take time for your spouse! Even a
minute or two can mean a lot and get you both
back on the same wavelength. I have found that
stopping to share a hug with my husband or to talk
for a few minutes can make a huge difference—
for him, for me, and for our baby.
—Heather Forrest

If you're fortunate to have in-laws close by, don't
be bashful—use them when they offer. Go out
on a date—lots of them—with your spouse. You
deserve it. We have one planned for Friday night!
—Toni Martucci

*Marriage is a lot like taking vitamins.
It's a process that involves the supplementation
of each other's minimum daily requirements.*

—Paul Newman

The best thing my husband and I did was to go on vacation a year after our second child was born. We left the children with my parents for ten days, which gave them quality time with their grandchildren. And it helped the children realize that "family" is more than just Mommy and Daddy. It's important to stay connected as husband and wife, even in the midst of another addition to the family. We came back fresh, re-energized, and ready to enjoy our children even more. We now try to take little husband/wife getaways twice a month.

—Angela Hughes

Mom and Dad, let your affection show. Your kids need to see that you love each other. Mom, go ahead and kiss your husband in front of the kids. Dad, sit on the couch with your wife and hold her closely. And when you argue, don't run off to the bedroom and fight behind closed doors. Kids need to know that people can love each other deeply and still disagree. When your children see that you still hold hands or kiss or hug after an argument, they learn that a disagreement doesn't mean that families fall apart. This really provides great security for your children.

—Erica Scott

Savor life's tiny delights—a crackling fire, a glorious sunset, a hug from your child, a walk with your husband or wife, a kiss behind the ear.

—John Anthony

Always remember to take a break and ask for help when needed. I am a 24-year-old, first-time parent and I have learned that when I feel like exploding it is okay to ask for help. Ask your husband to take over for a little while and take a hot bath or a walk. Anything—just relax! Your child will thank you and you'll feel much better.

—Anne M. Liston

Backyard romance: It was the middle of summer and our son was 9 months old. My husband and I wanted to sit out on our deck and enjoy the warm summer nights with our son—but he hated his playpen, and he couldn't be trusted to crawl around outside it. Our solution? We finally attached a tether rope to a walker. This allowed our son to walk a short distance in the yard on his own, but not get into trouble. He had a blast, and it was wonderful for my husband and me to have 30 minutes here and there to just relax and enjoy the summer sunsets.

—Kathleen Lyons

The family fireside is the best of schools.
—Arnold H. Glasow

Advice from a husband: If you're a new mother, just assume that your husband feels insecure about how to do even the basics with the new baby. Encourage rather than criticize. If your husband does something different from the way you do it— let it go if it's not hurting the baby. Later, after a lot of strokes, casually mention another way to do the task. Try not to be too territorial. Give your husband sole responsibility for the baby for short periods of time early on and try not to let on how anxious it makes you.

—Joel

I was given this advice when my wife was pregnant, and I felt I should pass it on. My wife chose to breast-feed our baby, so I knew that would be their special bonding time. In turn, we decided that bath time would my special time to bond. Bath time gives my wife a daily break to rest and be by herself, and it gives me the chance to do something nurturing for our baby—and to feel like something important is my job alone.

—Gregory P. Davis

We didn't have much, but we sure had plenty.
—Sherry Thomas

I have five kids, ages 8, 6 and 4, with 6-month-old twins which were a complete surprise. I am blessed with a wonderful, supportive husband who is very much my teammate. We routinely re-evaluate our parenting plan. What's working, what's not? Sometimes we involve the kids in the decisions. How can we be better parents? What are the areas they want to work on? It's a tricky job, always tweaking things here and there, but the result is worth it. Working together as a team, we have received the blessing of truly wonderful kids who love each other, respect others, and are a joy to be around.

—Kathy Escobar

My husband and I have alternated "shifts" with our son Aidan since he was born. I take the nights…and he takes the mornings. Aidan gets to bond with both of us…and we are able to give him the attention he needs without being all sleepy-eyed. We always walk in his room with a smile, and now that he is 2 months old and able to smile for other reasons besides gas, he wakes up with a smile, too!

—Kim Difederico

Never worry about the size of your Christmas tree. In the eyes of children, they are all 30 feet tall.

—Larry Wilde

As the mother of three, my advice is to keep a set daily routine—time for the kids, time for yourself in the afternoon, and quality time for husband and wife in the evening. Remember, there is no greater gift you can give your child than parents with a happy, healthy, and lasting marriage.

—Kelly Morgan-LaRosa

When our little girl was born, we only had a queen-size bed. There really wasn't enough room for my husband, myself, and our baby, so I asked my husband if he wanted me to sleep in the spare bedroom with our daughter. He replied that he wanted to be near us, so he moved the bed from our spare bedroom into our master bedroom. With two beds, we don't have a lot of room to walk around, but so what? We're together!

—Melissa Moffitt

Until recently, my husband and I shared a family bed with both our little sons, and I believe the experience enriched our bonds as a family. There is nothing more comforting in the world than cuddling up in your husband's arms with a sweet baby cuddled in yours. Infancy is a precious and fleeting miracle. Besides you can always have sex in the living room!

—Rose Sisneros

A truly rich man is one whose children run into his arms when his hands are empty.

—Pilar Coolinta

You stick together as husband and wife, and you stick together as father and mother, too. Here's what I think we did okay:

- Teach the kids to be honest, have a conscience, and do what's right.

- Believe in the child—their story is their truth. Teach respect by being respectful of their feelings.

- Listen to their stories of school, friends, etc. and be sincerely interested—it keeps the door open.

- Never ever tell their secrets.

- Don't try to be their best friend. Hold on tight, and let go little by little; too much freedom is not good.

- Do what is best for the child and not what the child wants—you are the parent.

- Reward for good behavior and use consequences for wrong behavior.

- Don't punish by word, but by action.

- Never give in on the critical points.

- Stay consistent; always do what you say.

—Laurie Escott

Family:
The original
Department of
Health, Education,
and Welfare.

—Peggy D'Marco

Having a baby is like taking your lower lip and forcing it over your head.
—Carol Burnett

Help for C-sections: My son was born in February, 1999. He was very big—10 pounds, 2 ounces—so I had a C-section. To recover, I drank fresh carrot juice (to heal from the inside out). I also put tea tree oil and vitamin E on the scar (to heal from the outside in). My doctor was blown away that I was completely healed in 10 days with virtually no scar.

—Stephanie Hall

Important safety tips for you and your little one: 1) Expect your baby to do the unexpected. Out of the blue they will learn to do things (such as rolling over and over off the bed), so be prepared. 2) Read ahead a few chapters in the development books and realize that your three-year-old may do the four-year-old stuff much sooner than expected. 3) Log onto childrecall.com and register all your baby's stuff—carseat, toys, pacifiers, etc.—anything that could be a risk. They will automatically contact you if there is a recall on some item that you might otherwise miss. 4) PLEASE take a CPR class for infants and children.

—Caron Wagner

If your newborn cries until he or she turns blue (like mine did), just blow gently on their face. They will look startled, but start breathing again!

—Chana Goldblatt

Your child is probably the most vulnerable while riding in an automobile. Please read the entire owner's manual for both your car AND your car seat to ensure your car seat is properly installed. If you're not absolutely certain you've done it right, contact your local police to have a Certified Car Seat Technician inspect your seat. If you're buying a new car, put your baby's car seat in the car you are considering and make sure it fits properly before you buy it. Don't use a car seat whose history you don't know, or if it has been in a previous accident, or is more than 5 years old. Be sure to register the purchase of your car seat with the manufacturer so they can notify you of any recalls. And by all means, protect yourself and buckle up, too!

—Debra Voegelin

It's very important you give
your children a chance.

—Nikki Giovanni

Beware of dogs! Teach your children early in life
to always ask your permission (and the owner's
permission) before petting a strange dog. Even
some of the nicest dogs may bite or snap at the
sudden approach of an excited child.

—Beth Keane

Try to reserve the word "NO" for emergencies
only. For example, "No, don't touch the stove!"
or "No! Stop!" For all other non-threatening
situations, simply say the child's name, followed
by "Please don't do that." Children respond
profoundly to the tone of your voice. Use a
forceful tone of voice when you say "No." Use
a disappointed tone when you say, "Please don't
do that." It is difficult to learn to reserve "No" for
emergencies only, but it becomes a potentially
life-saving signal between you and your child.

—Randee Meckley

My daughter loves opening our cabinets, but
we worry about what she might get into. To let
her explore cabinets without getting hurt, we chose
one cabinet and filled it with fun plastic containers
and put locks on the other cabinets. Now she can
explore "her" cabinet to her heart's content.

—Dawn Smith

*The simplest and safest toy,
one which even the youngest child can operate,
is called a grandparent.*

—Sam Levenson

A friend of mine had me buy a Baby-Safe Feeder (a netted feeder with a handle that baby holds). It helps prevent choking when baby eats cookies, etc. When she began teething, I put ice in the feeder and now she can't get enough! She can suck on the ice cubes while holding the handle of the feeder. I tried frozen watermelon pieces as well. This is a great product for teething babies!

—Nichole Galinkin

To soothe baby's teething pain, simply freeze some of those pre-packaged "tube yogurts." They are a healthy snack, great for sore gums and mommy's nerves, too.

—Carol Fuller

A local grandmother gave me this teething remedy: "In the old days we didn't have teething gels, we used good old vanilla." Just put a dab on your finger and rub it gently on your child's gums. My son loves the taste and it seems to give him just the right amount of relief until morning.

—Michelle Scott

Educate yourself about circumcision before
assuming that whatever is recommended to you
by friends and family is necessarily what's best
for your son. First research, then decide.

—John

I stopped breast-feeding my son at 9 months.
As soon as he started on whole milk he began
having chronic ear infections. At 22 months, on the
advice of my mother, I switched him to soy milk.
Within a week I noticed very obvious changes in
his personality. He stopped crying and seemed to
be a much happier child. Plus, the ear infections
virtually stopped. He is 6 years old today and still
drinks soy milk. If your child has any of these same
symptoms, you might check with your pediatrician
about a possible sensitivity to dairy products.

—Sharon Clark

Infant gas drops saved my sanity. What I thought
was colic was actually just gas!

—Celia Kotchounian

You've heard it before, but…never, ever leave your child alone in a car, bath, or around water, not even for an instant.

—Martha E. Teahan

Medicine syringes have been a lifesaver when giving my babies medicine. Baby can't spit medicine out from the syringe as easily as when given by spoon.

—Kelly Lewis

It was critical for our son to take a particularly bad-tasting medicine, but he couldn't get it down. A nurse gave us this tip: Just before giving your child the medicine, chill the dose in the freezer for a few minutes and then mix it with regular chocolate syrup. It works like a miracle. The cold numbs the taste buds and the chocolate syrup masks the taste. After the doses were all given, my son was still asking for chocolate syrup treats!

—Missy Earnest

Whenever a child falls, gets a bruise, or bumps his head, immediately apply Vaseline to the point of impact. It will minimize the discoloration of the bruise. It worked for Grandma—and it still works!

—Natalie Keller Morrison

When baby gets a cut, reach for the baby shampoo. Unlike regular soap, the no tears formula cleans your baby's cut without pain.

—Kim Lewis

Freeze a few of those little catsup or mustard packages that you get with your fast food. The next time your little one gets a bump or bruise, have your child hold one of the little frozen packages on their wound. This is so much neater and easier than a messy towel full of ice cubes—and the packages are just the right size for those little hands to hold.

—Jackie Bojesen

Any mother could perform the jobs of several air traffic controllers with great ease.

—Lisa Alther

Ice Pops work for anything! Keep a box in the freezer for sore throats, teething, dehydration, fevers, or whenever you need to encourage those liquids.

—Michelle Shoemaker

Baby powder is the "magic potion" that will remove wet sand from your child's body, pain-free.

—Jane Sweeney Beecher

If baby has a little splinter, simply apply Baby Orajel to the affected area. This will temporarily numb the skin so that you can use tweezers to pull the splinter out, and baby feels no pain!

—Kim Cammuso

I hang a stuffed bumblebee from the ceiling above the bathtub. When I have to rinse the shampoo out of my son's hair, I give the bee a little swing and I tell him to look up at the flying bumblebee—and then quickly pour the water over his head. It completely prevents shampoo in the eyes.

—Josie Bissett

Growing up ain't easy—
why do you think it takes so long?

— Tote Yamada

Beware of the sun! The latest guidelines
recommend protecting your baby's eyes from
direct sun at all times. (Sunglasses for 2-year-olds
are now available.) It goes without saying that
every parent should be in the habit of keeping
sunscreen on their children—and teaching them
to routinely apply it themselves as they get older.

— Beth Keane

Some of the best, cheapest—and safest—toys
you can offer your little one include everyday plastic
bottles, bowls, and lids—there's no weight, sharp
edges, or loose parts. Kids have great imaginations
and they love to make the noise!

— Michelle Barker Sybor

Delaney, our 16-month-old daughter, won't sit
still for her manicure. To avoid the possibility of
injuring her little fingers I keep a pair of baby nail
clippers and an emery board in both cars. Delaney
usually nods off in her car seat, so the moment
we pull safely into the driveway, I just give her
the manicure while she's still in dreamland.

— Sherri Viau

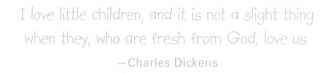

Always kiss your little one's boo-boos. It will
make you feel like their safe haven when they
come toddling over to you and ask, "Mommy, kiss
boo-boo?" Especially when you do and they say
"all better" and run off in search of more boo-boos.
It's just a small beginning to letting your child know
that they can always come to you with their
problems. That's how the trust begins.

—Cathy Halatek

When my 14-month-old son was a newborn, I
used to get extremely worried about every sniffle
or diaper rash that came our way. My sister-in-law
is an RN, and I used to call her in a panic for advice.
One night I called the hospital and spoke with a
nurse who was working with my sister-in-law that
evening. Hearing my panic, she calmly offered
me a "prescription" that will work for almost any
problem a mother might have. "Write this down
and tape it to your refrigerator and every mirror in
your home," she said. "It will help you through
anything: 'JUST LOVE HIM!'"

—Jenny Swenson

What can you do to promote world peace?
Go home and love your family.

—Mother Teresa

Treasure every healthy moment with your child—and keep him safe and close. As my mother used to say, "The gates of heaven are so easily found when we are little."

—Monica Smythe-Jarvis

Get a second opinion! Doctors are just people, and they sometimes make mistakes. As a parent, you can sense things about your children. If you sense that a doctor's diagnosis may be incorrect, seek a second opinion immediately.

—Ken Dorn

I am a 28-year-old single mother. My son, Devon, is 6 months old and has severe hemophilia. I have a lot to deal with right now, but I want to stop long enough to send this little reminder to all other parents. Take time each day to show your love to your kids in every way, and treasure the fact that they are healthy enough to do all the crazy, silly stuff they do. My son won't be able to participate in many sports, but I'm going to do whatever I can to give him a happy, normal life no matter what barriers I have to cross. The life and health of your little one is so precious...never take it for granted.

—Sharon Kermans

The best things you can give children, next to good habits, are good memories.

—Sydney Harris

*Each day of our lives we make deposits
in the memory banks of our children.*
—Charles R. Swindoll

Have fun with your kids, they need to know that Mom and Dad remember how! Take time to read to your child, no matter how busy you are. Give daily hugs and always let your child break free first!

—Lana Casto

From day one, have fun! During the first year try to get outside in the fresh air with your little one every day. When they are small, go out for walks with the stroller. Point out and name everything you see. When they are older and running around, go ahead and run with them. Get down and roll in the grass, jump in the puddles after the rain, and run around carefree with them. You won't believe how much fun you both will have!

—Amanda Henry

Listen to your children and marvel in the little things that catch their interest, like a train going by or a lizard on a tree. Have fun with your children, because they won't remember the nagging you might do, but they will remember when mom and dad play in a homemade tent with them!

—Rachel VanDemark

One of the most obvious facts about
grown-ups to a child is that they have
forgotten what it is like to be a child.

—Randall Jarrell

Interact with your child! Read, sing, get down on
the floor on your hands and knees and be part of
the action. Ask your child questions as you watch
her play. It is amazing how much they understand!
By watching my daughter play with her dolls, I have
learned that they love hugs and kisses just like
Mommy gives! In other words, I can see how I
parent by watching how my daughter interacts
with her dolls!

—Nicole Perkins

Make your child's room magical—it's easy. Hang
things from the ceiling (butterflies or mobiles); paint
their favorite characters on the walls; use stencils
to paint a sky, clouds, sun, moon and stars! Kids
love it! Their room should be a bright, safe place
for sleeping, learning and creativity—not a place
for punishment or time outs.

—Josie Bissett

Laugh, laugh, laugh! As the mother of two-year-
old twin boys I've had to learn to laugh when I
want to cry, scream, or just fall apart. It's hard to
remember that children are little and are just trying
to figure out this crazy world! Simple laughter can
transform a tense moment into a fun, bonding one.

—Annemarie Williams

86

You can do anything with children
if you only play with them.
—Gary Wells

If home is fun, children won't want to wander far from it. Discipline is important but so is playing with your children and having a great time!

—Trudy Davey

Here is my prescription for parents:

- Dance every day.
- Wrestle and let them win.
- Let them sleep in your bed.
- Buy the kids a vacuum; they love to vacuum.
- Film them 24 hours a day.
- Remember that every conversation with the young ones is one-sided—theirs.
- Never let them watch Barney because they will watch it constantly. (I blew it!)
- Save up and buy them the electric Jeep from Peg-Perego; it's hysterical to watch the older kids drive the little ones around.
- Let them run around naked.
- Feed the ducks as often as possible.
- And most of all, don't worry about spoiling your kids with toys. They lose interest in the new ones within 48 hours.

—Michael Greenberg,
President of Skechers USA

There would have to be something wrong with someone who could throw out a child's first Valentine card saying, "I love you, Mommy."

—Ginger Hutton

Vanna's Tips:

⭐ A fun idea for the kids in the bath or shower is to let them use a can of shaving cream. It's a little messy, but lots of fun—and what's wrong with fun?

⭐ When we receive a doll or stuffed animal from a friend, we always give it the name of that friend. For example, when Rosie gave my daughter a doll, we named her Rosie.

⭐ Always name and date the back of your photos. (C'mon, once and for all quit saying, "I will never forget when this happened.")

⭐ Always dilute baby's juice. My suggestion is one-fourth juice to three-fourths water.

⭐ Instead of juice all the time, there is nothing wrong with good old water! Help your babies get accustomed to the taste; otherwise they think that every drink must be sweet.

⭐ Instead of syrup, put applesauce on pancakes and waffles, or any fresh fruit such as strawberries or peaches.

—Vanna White

Grandchildren are so much fun, we should probably have them first.
—Anonymous

Ignore the dirty looks that some people will give you when your child is crying, throwing a tantrum, eating a Chicken McNugget, or wearing their rain boots on a beautiful sunny day. Look more carefully and you will notice another group of people—other parents—smiling, thinking, "been there, done that"—and not judging you in the least.

—Susan Pagano

Laugh at yourself, for if you can teach your children to do this, they will be happier, stress-free people when they grow up.

—Lori Green

Rigid schedules aren't for everyone. My four children (all under the age of 10) have learned to relax, have fun, and just "go with the flow." Go ahead and take a late-night trip to the supermarket when there are no crowds. Or take the family for a swim when most kids are going to bed. Who cares? Who says what a normal schedule is anyway? Someday, when your kids look back on their childhood with you, all the silly, unscheduled, spontaneous things will leap from their memories. Life's too short and too good to be scheduled.

—Erica Scott

You may have tangible wealth untold.
You may have caskets of jewels and coffers of
gold. But richer than I you can never be;
I had a mother who read to me.
—Strickland Gillilan

Build strong roots by surrounding your children with a solid family foundation that includes relatives, traditions, photos, and the passing down of customs, heirlooms, and sentimental items.

—Dionna Sanchez

I made a 60-minute video of my son Avery's entire first year of life. It included two-minute segments of his first Christmas, his first Father's Day, first Mother's Day, etc. To ensure that I could fit a year's worth of memories on just one tape, I kept each segment short and basically included JUST Avery. I concluded the video on his first birthday. By then, he was doing all sorts of tricks to add to the fun. At the end of the video, Avery was waving and saying "bye bye." I am so proud of this project. By having the date on each segment, you can see just how much he changed even over a couple of weeks.

—Molly Chunn

I keep a journal called, "Kids Say the Darndest Things." Every time one of the boys says something funny, I jot it down in the book.

—Alicea Nelson

Nobody can do for little children what grandparents do. Grandparents sort of sprinkle stardust over the lives of children.

—Alex Haley

Take a picture of your baby on the day he or she is born. Then take a picture on the same day for the next 12 months. At the end of the year, buy one of those 12-picture frames and you'll have a "first year" collage to treasure the rest of your life.

—Amy S. Davis

Buy those new picture frames that record little messages. We recorded our baby's laugh at 6 months. Just make sure your guests don't accidentally erase!

—Vonny Kleveland

I've had "discussions" with my son since he was 8 months old. How? We bought a couple of sign language books and made up some signs of our own. Now he is 15 months old and knows 26 signs. It's so much fun to know what he is thinking about before he can even put his thoughts into actual words!

—Teresa Bradshaw

Any adult who spends even fifteen minutes with a child outdoors finds himself drawn back to his own childhood, like Alice falling down the rabbit hole.

—Sharon MacLatchie

In preparation for a family vacation to visit relatives for the first time, I made a mini photo album for our son, Nicholas, with pictures of all the new relatives we would be seeing. He still loves this album over a year later.

—Elaine Renneberg

Make laminated placemats with pictures of his or her cousins, uncles, etc., so they will remember distant relatives.

—Kellie Tabor

Take lots of pictures, but don't just line up your kids and ask them to smile. Capture moments when they're unaware. Looking back, I find my favorites are the candid photos in which I was caught interacting with my three brothers. Now adults ourselves, we all have those photos in little frames throughout our houses. The formal "Holiday" pictures in which we are arranged neatly according to height aren't nearly as special as those where we're playing in our own little world together. As someone once said, "We do not remember days, we remember moments."

—Tote Yamada

You don't really understand human nature unless you know why a child on a merry-go-round will wave at his parents every time around—and why his parents will always wave back.

—William D. Tammes

Write notes to your children. Notes about how you feel about them. Write them down and just save them for when they're old enough to care. I started when my son was born, writing little notes to him in his baby book every few months, or when he did something really cute. Now they are like sweet little treasures in his baby book. Just reading and remembering the different stages is a joy. He loves for me to sit and read about when he was a baby. It's like his own little "story" of himself. It always brings tears to my eyes.

—Erica Scott

I write special stories and poems for each child. Sometimes they are about serious issues they are going through, and other times about silly things. I have also written an ABC book using family photos for each letter of the alphabet and a short description. All stories, poems and alphabet descriptions are easily composed on our home computer and then tucked in a binder, like a book. My kids love their "family books," and when they get older—what a keepsake!

—Donna Ozias

Having a young child explain something exciting he has seen is the finest example of communication you will ever hear or see.

—Bob Talbert

My mother died when I was 14. Since then, I have graduated from high school and college, gotten married, and had two wonderful boys. When I had my first child, I received a Baby Record book as a gift. As I was filling out the book, I realized that I knew very little about my own birth. Since my father left before I was 2, and my mother was deceased, I realized I would probably never find that information.

A year later, I was going through a box of my mother's things, and discovered that she actually had filled out a book about her first and only child, me. I was so thrilled! There was so much information in it. I was able to relate to my mom, as a mom myself, for the first time. I am so grateful that my mom took the time to fill that book out for me. Had she never found the time during those trying and exhausting months of my babyhood, I would never have had that information to pass on to my children. Therefore, I want to stress the importance of filling those books out with as much information as possible because you never do know what is going to happen!

—Lisa Sparks

There are no seven wonders of the world in the eyes of a child. There are seven million.

—Walt Streightift

Because we are a military family, we were unable to be close to home for my son Robert Anthony's first birthday. I decided to make him a "birthday quilt" that was created by the whole family. I sent squares of material to grandparents, great-grandparents, aunts, uncles, and cousins and asked that they each decorate their square with a first birthday wish for Robert. They could use embroidery, paint, markers, or crayons. Once their piece of the quilt was finished they sent it back to me and I sewed all the pieces together to make a quilt that he can have for a lifetime.

—Sherry Ann Sandoval

Make a time capsule! I made one for my son, Ethan, to be opened on his 18th birthday. In our time capsule are pictures of the family (including pets), pictures of our house and cars, magazines, and a local paper from the day he was born. We also made some predictions (how tall he will be, where he will go to college, etc.) and included his hospital blanket, cap, and bracelets! I think he will get a kick out of it and I am planning on making one for any future children.

—Alison Myers

If you can give your children only one gift,
let it be enthusiasm.

—Bruce Barton

Saying prayers with your children is one of the most meaningful things you can do. I started when my two youngest were about 2 years old, and years later it is a big part of our memories and our lives. Another piece of advice I have is to include a backrub after prayers. My 15-year-old son still loves it! It gives us special time to talk about what's going on in their lives.

—Charlotte Bezler

We lost my dad last November and it has been hard on my daughter. She was very close to her Pappa. He was actually visiting for her 5th birthday when he passed away. To help her cope with his death, we have created a wonderful photo album of memories for her. It is more like a scrapbook, as it contains birthday cards from Pappa, etc.—but placing them in the photo album pages makes it easier to turn. The album helps her feel closer to her grandfather, and makes it easier to talk about him.

—Bobbi Jo Innamorato Moran

I cannot forget my mother. She was my bridge. When I needed to get across, she steadied herself long enough for me to run across safely.

—Renita Weens

I am a mother of a beautiful 10-year-old daughter named Katie. We have always been very close to my mother (Katie's Nana). It's been wonderful having three generations close as can be, best friends even. When we found out my mother had cancer, Katie and I fell apart. Overnight she changed from really good girl, to really bad girl.

Finally my mother read a book to her. The book, by Maria Shriver, was about a little girl named Katie, whose grandmother was dying. My daughter felt that it was her. She even did a book report on it in school, which really touched our hearts. My mother passed away this past April, and Katie keeps that book next to her bed at night, along with my mom's picture, and a locket with a little bit of my mom's ashes in it, which says, "I love you always Katie—Nana." It's something that has touched my daughter's heart forever.

—Michele Solender

Don't be so full of adult there is
no room for the child in you.
—Bob Basso

As a child, I remember how important turning five-and-a-half or six-and-a-half was to me. As a mother, I will honor my son's half-birthdays by celebrating with half-cakes or half-cupcakes.

—Stephanie Delyea

Tuck a box of your baby's favorite toys in your cedar chest or attic, so he or she will have them to give to their own babies later in life.

—Heather Reynolds

When my daughters started reaching the age of puberty, I bought each of them a pair of earrings that would be "very special" to them. One daughter loves horses, so I bought her little gold "pony" earrings. On the first day of their first menstrual cycle I took each of them aside for a moment and presented the earrings as a small but meaningful celebration of their passage into womanhood.

—Sue McKone

> For children, play is serious learning.
> Play is really the work of childhood.
>
> —Fred Rogers

Do you live far away from your friends and relatives? My husband and I live outside of New York City, and my family is scattered all over the country. So, I created a website for my twin girls (www.devinetwins.com). This enables everyone in our extended family to keep up with the babies and see their progress. I can even share a steady stream of digitized baby pictures with everyone. It was very easy to do, and only costs $35 per year!

—Cary Beth Devine

Go visit your relatives—vacation time! Great "happy memory" moments happen on vacation. All work and no play makes us all grumpy, including the kids. Even if it's just a weekend trip, go somewhere and do something different! You never know when you're making a lifetime memory.

—Kathy Barr

A great way to thank friends and loved ones for gifts they give to your children is to take a picture of your child with their gift and send it in a Thank You card.

—Chrys Kimmel

The walks and talks we have with our 2-year-olds in red boots have a great deal to do with the values they will cherish as adults.

—Edith Hunter

Some parents bring their children up,
and some let them down.
—Carrie Sullivan

Everyone wants a loving, open, honest relationship with their child. If you want love, you must give love. If you want honesty, you must be honest. If you want openness, you must be willing to be open in return. These things work both ways. Your children can only be as open, honest, and loving as you are with them

—Kathleen Henderson

As my mother did for me, I always, always, listen to everything my child has to say, whether it's a truth, a made-up story, or just plain chatter. The day will come when your child will need to talk to you about something serious, and because you have always listened, they will always talk. Communication with your child opens the door to forever friendship.

—Kayleeana Marie Blake Wilson

Always keep in mind that you ARE the world to your little ones. The sun rises and sets on you. Always live by example, because they are always watching. To the world, you might be just one person, but to one person you might be the world!

—Jonelle Anderson

> We must convey to children
> that we believe in them.
>
> —Marian Wright Edelman

The day my son was born I witnessed a miracle, and at least once a day I make sure he sees himself as a miracle reflected in my eyes.

—Rob Estes

My favorite little bit of parenting advice to our kids, Tori and Randy, has always been, "Follow your dream. You may not achieve all of your dreams, but even if you achieve a part of your dream, you will be happy."

—Aaron Spelling, Producer

Live your life so that your children can tell their children that you not only stood for something wonderful—you acted on it.

—Dan Zadra

My three daughters are grown now, and between them I have been blessed with seven beautiful grandchildren. My advice is simple. Always remember that the job of a parent is to work yourself out of a job! Prepare your children well for life outside the home. Teach them to be honest, independent adults. I not only love my children and grandchildren, I LIKE them!

—Linda Jordan

I'm called a superstar. Heck, the real superstar is a man or woman who is raising six kids on $150 a week and teaching them good values.

—Spencer Haywood, NBA Forward

We can't depend entirely on the school system to teach our children. We are all teachers and have a lot to offer. No one will ever be able to give your child the attention that you can.

—Christine Eichmiller

We must teach our children to dream! I think the best way for my child to gain confidence in his own dreams is to watch his parents confidently pursue and achieve theirs. I am a young mother of a 19-month old boy, and I'm still in college studying to be a nurse. Many people discouraged my husband and me from getting married. They said I would never finish school, we wouldn't have any money and we'd have terrible jobs. Well, my grandmother always told me to follow my dreams. She praised me when others did not, and that is how I intend to raise my son.

Today my husband and I have our own home, and I will graduate from college this spring. Be a positive role model for your kids! Teach them to ignore negative feedback. Show them how to accomplish goals—not your goals, but theirs. That way, we all grow up happy and fulfilled.

—Kimberly Mason

Why do I have to be an example for your kid?
You be an example for your kid.
— Bob Gibson

I always told my son that he could be or do anything he wanted. Children live up to their parents' expectations. If you tell them they are wonderful, they will be. If you tell them they are stupid or put them down—sure enough, that's what they are likely to become.

— Gramma Marie Estes

Get involved in your kids' sports activities—if not coaching, being on the sidelines for every event you possibly can. Don't emphasize the winning or the scoring, but give accolades for good sportsmanship and teamwork. And whatever you do, don't embarrass your kids by throwing a temper tantrum at the referees or coaches!

— Grandpa Bill Mann

Children will adopt the value system of the adults around them. Good sound morals are "caught not taught." You cannot teach a child to be honest and truthful if you, yourself are not so. Model yourself after the kind of person you want your child to become. Our children may not always do what we say, but they inevitably do what we do.

— Grandma Roni Bissett, author of
"Don't Trip Over the Pebbles in Your Life."

Sometimes the poorest parents leave their children the richest inheritance.

—Ruth Renkel

Discipline your children with positive love and encouragement; don't break their spirit with negative love and discouragement.

—Michael

When you feel the urge to yell or otherwise "lose it" with your child, always stop and look at the situation through your little one's eyes. It always works for me. We end up actually talking it out, or playing, or mixing play with discipline. No one is perfect, including, and especially, a parent.

—Carey Magee Goffman

Before I had kids I vowed never to be "that kind of mother." Well, now that I have two daughters I understand where those mothers are coming from—it's so easy to lose your patience and perspective. So each day I take a moment to remind myself of two little words—love and gratitude. Children truly are a gift from God. They are not just the little challenges we must deal with day-to-day; they are the reason we are here day-to-day. Children's spirits are so very fragile. As parents we need to recognize this and treat them, not simply as our children—but as our treasures.

—Michele Florence

Listen to the mustn'ts, child, listen to the
don'ts—listen to the shouldn'ts, the impossibles,
the won'ts—listen to the never haves, then
listen close to me—anything can happen, child.
ANYTHING can be.

—Shel Silverstein

I was only 18 when my daughter, now two-and-a-half, was born, and I thought I knew everything about being a mommy. I grew up being yelled at by my parents, so naturally that's how I started to raise my daughter. One day, after I yelled at her for not coming in the house, her eyes started to water, her nose turned red, and she sobbed, "I'm so sorry, Mommy." I knew right then that I didn't know as much as I thought.

Now each morning I look at her and silently remind myself that she is a treasure. I have learned to listen carefully to my daughter, take a deep breath, talk in soothing tones, explain patiently, ask questions, get her opinion, and we laugh together, and SHE LISTENS! She is the light of my life. No, I don't know everything about being a mommy, but I do know that the cycle of yelling that has been in my family will stop with me and my daughter.

—Amelia Zindros

A child is not a vase to be filled,
but a fire to be lit.
—Rabelais

I am a new mom who had been trying to get pregnant for quite a while, and now I am blessed with a beautiful, sweet little girl. My parents were screamers who never showed any display of affection—and I vowed to set a better example for my daughter. Here are the guidelines I have set for myself: Never fight in front of your children. Always show love to your spouse and a united front on issues concerning your children. Each day, tell your child what a blessing they are and point out something special about them. Be a parent, not just a friend, to your child. Designate a special day for your child. My husband says that he wants to have a regular father/daughter day, where they can go to lunch at the park and play together. Oh, how wonderful, since I didn't have that!

—Cheryl Claes

Love them unconditionally and let them know how special they are by praising all their positive behaviors, no matter how small you might think they are. It is special to a child to be told how pretty, smart, good, fun, wonderful, or special they are.

—JoLee Stanneart

He taught me to run high on my toes.
I will always remember his words:
"Run proud and remember you are alive."

—Brian Andreas, "Still Mostly True"

I had six children. One day one of my little girls
was really misbehaving and probably deserved a
spanking. Instead I took her little hand and walked
her to her room; she felt warm, so I held her in my
arms and rocked her. I soon realized that she was
not feeling well, so I put a cold washcloth on her
forehead, rocked her some more and sang a little
song to her. To this day, my little girl (who is now
35 and has a little girl of her own), remembers
what I did that day. Consider this little story the
next time your child appears to deserve a spanking.

—Lena Stuber

Show them you love them, even when you think
they deserve it least!

—Gene Juarez

Instead of taking it out on your little one, just
laugh it off. Besides, that expensive lipstick that
looked so dazzling on you actually does look better
on that devilish cherubic face, and not all that bad
on the wall!

—Tracy Jordan

The best inheritance a father can give his children is a few minutes of his time each day.

—O.A. Battista

I'm a young mother of two very active little boys. I've found that the "terrible twos" may last well into the third year. At times I feel like I'm failing, especially when my boys get too bold. Then, I remember, "Hey, they're kids. They are not supposed to be perfect—they are just supposed to be loved!" Well, that's your job and mine. Just be their "best friend." Comfort them. Your eyes and face are a mirror for them, so never let them see you worry. Always be reassuring and loving, with a warm hug and a smile, and all their troubles will disappear into your arms.

—Carly Jopling

My 3-year-old son, Marshall, stripped every flower out of my garden this year. Every time a new flower bloomed, he brought it right in, announcing he had a SURPRISE for me! My husband suggested we urge him not to pick the flowers—but I didn't have the heart. He got such pleasure from bringing them to me. I always hugged him and told him how beautiful they were while putting them in a nice vase. Who knows if next year he will still do the same thing, but it is my gift to him to accept the flowers unconditionally.

—Mary Pokrentowski

Parents need to fill a child's bucket of self-esteem so high that the rest of the world can't poke enough holes in it to drain it dry.

—Alvin Price

The best advice I have ever heard was Oprah Winfrey quoting Maya Angelou, who said that the thing she wished for most as a child was for her parents' eyes to light up when she walked into the room. That simple statement changed the entire way I relate to my 15-month-old twins. Now I always make sure that I look right at them and smile the moment I see them.

—Lynn Weber

I love my mom's favorite piece of advice: "Most people don't realize how easy it is to make someone else happy!" Just think of our own children. You really have been given a chance to improve this world with your newest addition! Never lose sight of the fact that it is so wonderfully easy to brighten a child's day (and night, if they opt to keep you up at all hours). Nothing is more satisfying as a new parent than knowing in your heart that you are deserving of your child's love and affection because of all the energy, creativity, and love that you are willing to expend each and every day and night! We're all worth the effort, especially our children...don't you think?

—Dianna Hunt

My father's quiet example lit up
my life and our town.
—Carol O'Leary

I'm a child psychologist, the mother of four, and the grandmother of eight. My suggestion is to talk about your children to other adults—and let your children hear it. This leaves a very powerful impression on kids. What will you say? Just be sincere. Simply observe and then talk about your children's positive qualities. Example: "Gee, I'm so proud of Mary. She's such a hard worker, so kind, shares with others, is such a good thinker, etc."

—Dr. Sylvia Rimm, Author of "How to Parent so Children will Learn" and "See Jane Win"

If you want them to listen to you, listen to them. If you want them to read, read to them—and let them see you read.

—Grandpa Larry Estes

Our family plays a self-esteem game called, "Positive Roundtable." We all sit in a circle around the dinner table, and then take turns relating something positive about every other member. As I say in my book, "Mommy Magic", I believe that a little magic is sprinkled into the heart of every mother when a child is born. The challenge is keeping that magic alive on a daily basis.

—Adria Manary

A grandparent's love is very special. My grandmother taught my brothers and me that we should always be there for our family. She would say that people come and go in our lives, but your family is there forever. My grandmother's home was always open to us, day or night. She made us feel that we were the most important people in the world to her and that loving us was a gift she would never take for granted. She was our safety net and our space to share all the good things in life. Because of her love, my brothers and I grew up knowing how special we are.

—Kim Blazonczyk

If you have a Grandma who lives nearby and you have a baby who is having nighttime feedings, consider giving Grandma the privilege of taking over the feedings one or two nights a week. From experience I know that the time spent provides a wonderful bonding opportunity for Grandma and Baby—and it also gives mom and dad a much-needed rest.

—Gramma Judy

You must believe in yourself, my child, or
no one else will believe in you. Be self-confident,
self-reliant, and even if you don't make it, you will
know you have done your best. Now go to it.

—Mary Hardy MacArthur

As a child I always suffered from terrible
separation anxiety. One of the most wonderful
things my mother did to help me cope was to dab
a bit of her perfume on my wrists each morning
before nursery school. Whenever I found myself
sad and lonely, I could smell her scent upon my
skin and feel her with me. Now, as a college
student, I keep a bottle of her scent with me, to
spray whenever I need her company. It's an
ageless Mommy tip!

—Alexandra Asher-Sears

When I was a little girl my grandmother told
me, "Love can never be taken away—it can only
be divided." I never felt alone in my family, I always
felt unconditionally loved—and I want my own
children to have that same gift.

—Cullen Renee' Ard

> One of the luckiest things that can happen to you
> in life is to have a happy childhood.
>
> —Agatha Christie

I raised a foster daughter, and when she was around 7 she started having nightmares and had to sleep with the light on in her room. I would tuck her in every night and read her a story. We would talk for a little while (I would answer questions about life), she would say a prayer for her family, and I would try to comfort her. But nothing seemed to help; the nightmares continued. Then I had an idea. I got a little paper angel and I hung it right over her bed, above her head, and I explained to her that we all have a Guardian Angel watching over us every day and night. I told her that this was her Guardian Angel, and that she would be protected all night while she slept. The nightmares stopped and she no longer had to sleep with the light on. At last she felt safe.

—Belinda Stewart

At bedtime be alert to the magic in your sleepy child. One night my 6-year-old asked me to leave the light on in her room. I thought she was frightened, so I assured her it was okay to turn off the light because I would be right down the hall if she needed me. "No, Daddy," she smiled, "I'm not afraid. Angels are attracted to the light."

—Don Ward

*The future of the world would be assured
if every child were loved.*

—Bernie Siegel

Even though your kids are not small any more, and can't sit on your lap, they still need lots of hugs, kisses, and "I love you's". Most of all, they need your undivided attention and time.

—Melissa

I was the youngest of nine children (five adopted, me being one of them) and now I am a 31-year-old mother of three and a step-mom to two. The very best "little bit of wisdom" I can offer is…never lose the cuddle time. Take 15 minutes out of your busy day—every day—to just cuddle your children and listen to them.

—Elizabeth P. Wood

My son Jacob, age 5, and I cuddle in bed every morning and it makes a wonderful start to any day. In the evening, we cuddle with his daddy too. One of these days I know he will not want to do this anymore, so I am taking full advantage of it now.

—Michele Langlais

*The most important thing that parents can teach
their children is how to get along without them.*
—Frank Clark

Each night, as my children, Shana and Mason
(ages 4 and 2), are lying in bed, I ask them to
describe the happiest and saddest parts of their
day. It is absolutely amazing what you can learn
about your children in those few precious
moments. It gives you a treasured glimpse into
their hearts and minds—something that is often
hard to capture in the daily routine of poopy diapers
and crayon on the walls. Even a small child who
can barely talk will feel valued knowing that Mom
cares about his or her feelings.

—Patty Smith

Never underestimate the wisdom or fresh
perspective your child can share with you. Every
night my 2-year-old needs to tell the beautiful moon
goodnight. Seeing things through his eyes gives
me a better idea of what I could be missing!

—Gina Frerichs

Try to see things through your child's eyes. You'll
be amazed how you can rediscover the world and
what a beautiful place it can be, not to mention
how fun it can be for you both. It gives you the
chance to be a kid again!

—Jonelle Anderson

A torn jacket is soon mended;
but hard words bruise the heart of a child.
—Henry Wadsworth Longfellow

Bedtime, or any time, is the best time to praise your child. They yearn for your approval. Whether they have straight F's or straight A's, they still need encouragement. Every day let them know that they are capable of doing the impossible and, no matter what happens, don't ever lose faith in them!

—Jessica McKinney

Be a good-finder! Constantly be on the look-out for the good things your child is doing every day. Try to catch them red-handed in the act of doing something right—and then praise them for it! I read a statistic once that said that eight out of ten messages that our kids hear each day are negative or non-supportive. "Pick up your clothes...don't slam the door...why are you so lazy?" We don't mean to talk to our kids this way— we just fall into the habit—but it's an easy habit to break! One of my favorite quotes is, "Praise is nothing more than letting off a little esteem." It only takes a moment for you and me to sincerely praise our kids for doing something right—but I think those little moments pile up into a lifetime of good feelings, confidence and self-esteem.

—Bob Moawad,
National Association for Self Esteem

My advice to mothers with sons is to never hold back on your affection—go ahead and kiss, hug, and love them openly all through their teens and beyond. As the mother of two boys, I was concerned that they would be raised with a sensitivity toward others. From a very young age, when something happened to them, I would say, "How did that make you feel?" or "That must have been scary or sad or wonderful." When our oldest was about 14, I overheard him say to one of his friends, "I'm sorry that happened to you. I can see why you're so sad." And now at almost 17, he senses when I've had a bad day and will say, "Sit down, tell me about it." There is nothing more wonderful than having your 6-foot son come up and put his arms around you with a "How's it goin', Mom?"

—Julie Battle

Every day, let your child know that, no matter what, you are behind him or her one hundred percent. As they grow older, pick your battles wisely. Don't worry if he/she wants to wear the jeans with the ripped knees—after all, that's not the end of the world, so just worry about the things that will be harmful. "Mother" is the greatest title any woman can ever earn in life!

—Dina Roventini

Children are likely to live up to
what you believe of them.
—Lady Bird Johnson

Hugs are Band-Aids for a child's spirit.

—Suzanne Johnson

When you say goodnight to your children, always
look them in the eye and say, "I love you"—and
don't forget the kiss!

—Natalie Wazana

My advice is to always end the day by telling
your children, "I love you"—no matter what
happened throughout the day.

—Cindy Ryan

Love and kiss and hug your child whenever you
want—even wake the baby with a kiss if you want
to. You may not be blessed with another.

—Martha E. Teahan

Turn around and
you're two, turn around
and you're four,
turn around and
you're a young girl
going out of my door.

—Malvina Collins, "Turn Around," 1958

We had a disappointing experience with our children—they all grew up.
—Leslie Bonaventure

Never forget that your children are special little treasures, given to you by God, on loan for a limited amount of time.

—Nina LaRue

When you are prioritizing, remember that your children are ALWAYS Number One.

—Melissa Jones

The dirty dishes and laundry will always be there tomorrow, but your child may not. So for those who thrive on organization and total control in life, allow yourself the time and privilege every day of getting to know your little one and letting them get to know you. Remember it was said, "Tomorrow is another day." So let a little bit of every today be the yesterday you made the most of, and the tomorrow that you look forward to doing all over again.

—Shelley Yeatts

Our children are living messages we send to a time and place we will never see.

—Anonymous

When I became a stay-at-home mother to my first born son, Jack, I believed I could still keep my home spotless. While I was rushing around doing the laundry, dishes, vacuuming, etc., my son would get rather fussy. I found that if I just sat with him and watched him play, he would stop fussing. He just wanted a little attention! My husband and I decided to hire a housekeeper to deep clean our house every two weeks. I know that seems like a luxury for a one-income family, but it really isn't that expensive and it has paid off for our family in so many ways.

—Natalie Kelley

The best advice I can give is to try to have fun with it all—because childhood doesn't last forever. Through all the commotion that happens with my little ones each day I try to remember that my children are only young once. Let your older children help out in any way, but remember to spend time with the older child when the baby is sleeping or playing. Each one of your children will teach you something new if you just let them. They have the most wonderful jobs in the world— "just being a kid."

—Chris Milawski

Children are more in need of models than of critics.
—Carolyn Coats

Children grow up so fast and then one day—
Poof!—they're gone. Here's a poem I framed to
remind my husband and me of the important role
we play in our little boy's life:

"There are little eyes upon you
and they're watching night and day.
There are little ears that quickly
take in every word you say.
There are little hands all eager
to do anything you do;
and a little boy who's dreaming
of the day he'll be like you.
You're the little fellow's idol,
you're the wisest of the wise.
In his little mind about you
no suspicions ever rise.
You are setting an example
every day in all you do,
for the little boy who's waiting
to grow up to be like you."

—Michelle and Dan Perry

Let your children go if you want to keep them.
—Malcolm Forbes

Love leaves the dust in search of a child's laugh.
Love smiles at the tiny fingerprints on a newly
cleaned window.
Love wipes away the tears before it wipes up the
spilled milk.
Love picks up the child before it picks up the toys.
Love is ever-present through the trials.
Love reprimands, reproves, and is responsive.
Love crawls with the baby, walks with the toddler,
runs with the child, then stands aside to let the
youth walk into adulthood.

—Unknown

Life, Love, Children and Grandchildren.
The love between a father and child, and a
mother and child, is forever. This kind of love is
unconditional. Interweave it with understanding,
patience, and respect. Fill it with traditions,
memories, and dreams. Give Love, receive
Love. Give a smile, take a hand.

—Joe and Linda Heutmaker

You gave me wings, now let me fly!
—Don Ward

My advice, as obvious as it is, came to me only after a very sad period. I am the mother of two, but I lost my first son, Stefano, when he was only 20 months old to a congenital heart defect. Throughout the 20 months we had together, Stefano appeared to be perfectly healthy, and I thought I would have him forever. I was always one to think of the future, constantly planning for tomorrow, and seldom appreciating today. Stefano taught me that tomorrow might not come and that today is what we have. To all parents, I offer this gentle reminder: Please don't focus so much on the future that you neglect the beauty and promise of the here and now. I was blessed with another boy, Nicolas, 18 months later. Nicolas has benefited from this simple insight.

—Arielle Leone

Don't wish this incredible experience away. Stop saying, "I can't wait until he can hold his bottle" or, "Life will be so much easier once she is walking." Savor every single moment—before you know it, you will have wished your baby into an adult.

—Laura Ping

Your children are always your babies,
even if they have gray hair.
—Janet Leigh

Just remember that the housework and other chores or errands will always wait! Read that book when they ask, or lie in bed with them those last few minutes. Time spent with your children is so precious. Don't let tomorrow rob you of today!

—Danna Fleming

Put down the mop, leave the dirty dishes in the sink, leave the dirty clothes in the laundry, turn off the TV, and let the phone ring. Pick up your child right now and go outside and make pictures out of the clouds. Tomorrow may come, but you can never get today back.

—Brenda Stier

Take good care of yourself so you can live a long life. To see your children and grandchildren become adults is a joy, but to watch your great grandchildren grow up is the ultimate happiness!

—Gramma Donna Heutmaker

On Judgment Day,
if God should say,
"Did you clean your
house today?"
I will say, "I did not...
I played with
the children
and I forgot."

—Sue Wall

Send us your Little Bits!

We are currently planning new editions of *Little Bits of Wisdom* and invite you to contribute yours. Just visit our website today. Thank you for your contribution: www.littlebitsofwisdom.com

To order additional copies of *Little Bits of Wisdom*, or to receive a free catalog of Compendium products, call or write today:

COM·PEN´·DI·UM™
Incorporated

Publishing and Communications

*E*nriching the lives of millions, one person at a time.

This book may be ordered directly from the publisher, but please try your local bookstore first!

Call toll free (800) 91-IDEAS
6325 212th St. SW, Suite K,
Lynnwood, WA 98036

www.compendiuminc.com